RECORD KEEPING AND ARCHIVES IN WEST GERMANY

by

Maralyn A. Wellauer

Roots International
3239 North 58th Street
Milwaukee, Wisconsin 53216

International Standard Book Number 0-932019-10-2

CONTENTS

PREFACE

In 1976, I published a compendium entitled, A
GUIDE TO FOREIGN GENEALOGICAL RESEARCH: A SELECTED
BIBLIOGRAPHY OF PRINTED MATERIAL WITH ADDRESSES.
The great demand for this title was traced mainly
to the interest in the sections dealing with
research in German-speaking countries.

After AGTFGR was allowed to go out-of-print
two years following its release, TRACING YOUR
GERMAN ROOTS was issued. The first guide of its
kind, the small book proposed all- purpose
solutions to problems like finding an ancestor's
place of origin in Germany and pursuing the search
for documentation through the mail. The time came,
in 1987, when a decision had to be made on whether
a second, revised and enlarged edition of the work
would be undertaken. It was then decided to pursue
a new concept. A fresh, new series of three
volumes would supercede TRACING YOUR GERMAN ROOTS.
While still striving to maintain a similiar spirit
of self-help and education, the new volumes would
serve an even wider audience of genealogists and
family historians, and to tackle the subjects
perceived to be of greatest interest.

It is not cost or space effective, to produce
a comprehensive guide to German research. It is
wiser, in the opinion of this author, for example,
to provide researchers interested in the areas now
part of the German Democratic Republic with their
own volume, rather than to squeeze in a few pages
as an afterthought in a book with a wider range of
topics. Hence, the volume, FAMILY HISTORY RESEARCH
IN THE GERMAN DEMOCRATIC REPUBLIC, Milwaukee, 1987.

Also, it is unconscionable to combine in one
volume a commentary on DOING YOUR HOMEWORK ON A
GERMAN IMMIGRANT ANCESTOR, together with
intermediate and advanced research methodology,
hence another volume in the series (forthcoming in
1988).

This volume, RECORD KEEPING AND ARCHIVES IN
WEST GERMANY (FRG), deals specifically with the
records and archives located in the Federal
Republic of Germany. With this volume, users should
be able to apply new knowledge to their own
research programs, by determining what records are
extant for a specific locality; the time period
covered by these sources; and what genealogical
information these records contain. Information on

where these records are available is given with addresses for correspondence directly with the appropriate repositories are provided.

Maralyn A. Wellauer
Milwaukee, Wisconsin
October, 1987

INTRODUCTION

The complexities surrounding the historical background and geography of the former German Empire present special obstacles to the genealogist. Particularily formidible is the considerable size of the area covered by the Empire. It was large, incooperating a number of provinces which extended over a substantial portion of Central Europe. Today, these regions belong to the independent nations of the Federal Republic of Germany (FRG), the German Democratic Republic (GDR), Poland, Czechoslovakia, and others.

Numerous political divisions made their appearance on maps of Germany before the Confederation of the States in 1871. The largest of these were the kingdoms of Prussia, Bavaria, Wuerttemberg and Saxony, which covered the majority of the Empire. There were the Grand Duchies of Baden, Hesse, Mecklenburg-Schwerin, Mecklenburg-Strelitz, Oldenburg and Saxe-Weimar. The Empire also included numerous Duchies, Principalities, and Free Cities.

Changes in administration of the various states led to a multitude of place-name changes in past centuries. A conservative estimate might indicate that approximately 70% of the road blocks encountered in researching German families can be attributed to the incorrect identification of place names.

Not only can we consider the extent of the German states and territories overwhelming, but in addition, changes in administration, boundary disputes and religious conflicts have affected the condition of material of genealogical value and other historical materials surviving in archives today. Additional problems can be traced to the frequency of war-like activities which devasted areas to varying degrees since the Thirty Years War (a major period of concern for the genealogists). Bombing raids, fire storms, and bombings of World War II, which occurred more recently, are blamed for the destruction of valuable genealogical material which survived past centuries.

Occasionally, progress on a lineage is halted due to the destruction of records, or of their alleged destruction. Many inquiries to Germany are still answered by saying that records were destroyed in the war and are unavailable. In general, preparations to move valuable material were made when the unrest in Europe began and rumors that war was imminent were realized, so it is highly unlikely that all the excuses ring true. These stories of "missing books" may have the same frequency as those in the United States concerning the "burned courthouses" in southern counties. To find out if this is a ruse, one can check inventories of the WPA (Works Progress Administration) which will yield clues to what was destroyed after the Civil War, what was kept originally, and what was thrown out. In the same manner, early German archive inventories can be matched against the contents of more recent compilations to determine extant material.

REPOSITORIES

REPOSITORIES

Thousands of important source records, manuscripts and other papers pertaining to former German citizens are scattered in repositories located all over Germany, the United States and the world. They are located in hundreds of national, regional and local archives, each having free to limited accessibility to genealogists.

There has never been a central repository for genealogical material in German history. No office even roughly compares in function with the National Archives or Library of Congress in Washington, D.C. or with any individual state's vital statistics (or Board of Health) offices.

Perhaps the closest thing to a central repository of German parish and civil records exists under the auspices of the Church of Jesus Christ of Latter-Day Saints (LDS or Mormon Church), 35 North West Temple Street, Salt Lake City, Utah, 84150. For more than forty years, microfilm teams have been gathering copies of original source records from German repositories and storing them near Salt Lake City.

In 1980, a guide to the LDS German collection was released: Smelser, Ronald, et al. PRELIMINARY SURVEY OF THE GERMAN COLLECTION, University of Utah Press, Salt Lake City, 1979. The strength of the collection lies in the areas of Rheinland-Pfalz, Nordrhein and Baden-Wuerttemberg.

Particularily valuable for family researchers is the International Genealogical Index (IGI) which provides dates of christenings, marriages and burials for a large number of individuals of German origin. Many have been included as the result of the Controlled Extraction Program, where members have extracted the names and dates from the actual parish registers and submitted them for inclusion on the IGI.

The library also has an unsurpassed collection of secondary source material, parish register abstracts, transciptions and transcipts. (See the volume on DOING YOUR HOMEWORK ON A GERMAN IMMIGRANT ANCESTOR for a more complete explanation of the Mormon facilities.)

It is always necessary to know as much as possible about an immigrant before writing to or visiting Germany. To maintain a successful search, through overseas repositories, the researcher must maintain the ability to identify each ancestor with respect to his or her full name, date of an event important in their life while in Europe, and a place where that event occurred. When one of these elements is lost, great difficulties will be encountered. Since the location of German populations has been unstable for centuries, genealogists may find it necessary to pursue their quest in more than one archival repository.

War and other catastrophes motivated the German people to become mobile. Migrations became an important part of the history of Europe for hundreds of years. There were a variety of reasons for people moving from place to place but the major motivations were backed by religious, economic, social or religious situations. Families were displaced by multiple wars and conflicts; moved in search of food; by deprivation during natural disasters and famines; a need for jobs, and so on. Regardless of the reason, time period or destination, the result of the migration was the displacement of the population, either temporarily or permanently, to distant and unfamiliar new lands. The German people were involved in many internal migrations to satisfy their needs.

In addition to the influence exerted upon genealogy by historical and geographical factors, the results of a careful search in Germany are, for the most part, also continent upon the organization and administration of various types of archives. All of the German repositories are characterized by distinctive, individual features, and identifiable by specified holdings, specialities, sources and foundations. Even as the manner of current administration may be responsible for the success or failure of an inquiry, the method of past control has had its effect on the outcome of a search.

German archives can be classified according as to their general jurisdictional authority, structurally as follows:

State Archives (Staatsarchive) (Landesarchive)

State archives contain extensive collections of materials pertaining to provincial matters. These archives can be found throughout Germany. The number of repositories of this type range from one in the smaller states to several in the larger ones, such as the former Kingdoms of Prussia and Bavaria. Documents concerning domestic and foreign affairs of state and government; economic and religion; and social issues are on deposit in individual locations. (See Appendix A)

Municipal or City Archives (Stadtarchive)

Many German cities of substantial size or importance have collections of material pertaining to the legislation and administration of their municipality. These collections are not representative of as large an area as those records kept in the state archives. In many of the Stadtarchive, these records may pre-date the thirteenth century, with some of the earliest in print. Some of the source material maintained includes guild records, city chronicles, notarial books, citizenship rolls, land records, probate files, etc.

The number of municipal archives throughout Germany is very large and the collections vary greatly in character and value. To fully utilize the materials in each area, one must study available inventories and descriptive guides, many of which are in US libraries or can be ordered through inter-library loan.

Because the total number of Stadtarchive is in the hundreds, no attempt will be made here to enumerate them all. All too often, omissions would be obvious, and this would be virtually unavoidable. Instead, a few comments on the correct procedure for locating this information for a particular community should prove helpful.

MEYERS ORTS-UND VERKEHRSLEXIKON DES DEUTSCHEN REICHS, an important reference for determining the correct place names of German communes, will also be invaluable for finding Standesamt (Civil Registry) offices. Smaller towns and villages may be under the juridication of a single Standesamt located miles away. To find the locality, first determine which town your ancestors came from. The entry for that community will show the civil, political, ecclesiastical and military districts to which it belongs. You will be able to determine if the community had its own Standesamt by the abbreviation, StaA. If it is punctuated by a comma or a semicolon, that means the place has its own Standesamt. If neither mark appears after the StdA, the entry will give the name of the place where the civil registry for the commune is located, which is

the next town listed followed by a comma or a
semicolon.

    Once the location of the Standesamt is found,
one may consult the POSTLEITZAHLENVERZEICHNISSE
(Postal Code Book) to determine the four digit code
to formulate the address. This small, inexpensive
volume, available from the Postamt in Koeln
(Cologne), contains the zip codes for each
community in the Federal Republic of Germany and
also for the German Democratic Republic.

    To contact the civil registry office of a
community directly, one can address a letter as
follows:

        Standesamt
        D-_____ (4 digit postal code + town name)
        Federal Republic of Germany

        Standesamt
            DDR-_____(4 digit postal code + town
        name)
        German Democratic Republic

Church   Archives   (Kirchenarchive)
(Kirchenbuchstelle) (Landeskirchenarchive)

    During the 19th century, several confessions,
i.e. Catholic, Lutheran, Reformed, etc. established
a number of ecclesiastical archives and began
collecting documents and papers of a general nature
relating to church affairs. This included record
books from individual parishes only when they were
deposited voluntarily. Gradually, during the past
century, church archives accumulated originals,
duplicates and transcriptions of baptismal,
marriage and burial entries from local parish
administrators. It wasn't until recently that the
advantages of separate archives for church
materials have became clear to genealogists.

    The effect of the consolidation of religious
materials was to provide standardized access to
parish registers. It encourages researchers to
forward inquiries to a central office rather than
to parishes scattered throughout an ecclesiastical
district. If research is done in person, a visit to
a central repository makes motoring to various
parsonages unnecessary. This represents a savings

in time and makes it unnecessary to schedule appointments to meet pastors at a variety of sites. If the original registers or transcripts are not in an area repository, the individual parish can be contacted. More will be said about that process later.

Researchers can generally expect to be welcomed with a varying degree of receptiveness when dealing with individuals, so it is difficult to predict the outcome of a personal encounter when so many variables are involved. Church archives provide procedures for the use of collections and charge for services rendered to researchers according to the amount of time and labor spent. Inquiries are handled in a standardized way.

A summary of some of the area repositories for church books by region:

a) Baden - Protestant books - Karlsruhe
        Catholic   "   - Freiburg

b) Bavaria - Catholic Books - Regensburg, Muenich, Augsburg, Bamberg, Eichstaett, Passau, Wuerzburg

c) Hannover - Catholic Books - Hildesheim, Osnabrueck

d) Hessen-Darmstadt - Protestant Books - Darmstadt
                    Catholic " - Fulda, Mainz

e) Hessen-Nassau - Catholic Books - Limburg

f) Mecklenburg - Lutheran Books - Ratzeburg

g) Pomerania - Some Lutheran Books - Greifswald and Berlin (Jebenstrasse 3)

h) Posen - some Catholic Books - Regensburg (F.R.G) Some in Poland and some in Berlin

i) East and West Prussia - Lutheran Books - Berlin or Poland

j) Saarland - Catholic Books -Trier
            Protestant Books - Speyer

(Also see Appendix B & C for addresses)

Some state archives (Staatsarchive) have solicited collections of duplicate church books from within their regions. For instance, the

Staatsarchiv in Darmstadt (D-6100) has duplicates of both Catholic and Protestant church books from the 19th century.

In addition to the archives of the states and communes, Germany has many other types of archives. For example, there are Nobility Archives (Adelarchive), Family Archives (Familienarchive), Military or Federal Archives (Bundesarchive or Heeresarchive), University Archives (Universitaetsarchive), scientific archives, industrial and institutional archives, and media archives, to name some of the more visible special function centers.

ORGANIZATION
OF THE
ARCHIVES

ORGANIZATION OF THE ARCHIVES

Each archive establishes their own set of well-defined rules for the use of the material commanded to their protection. Some offices are well staffed and therefore have more time to provide answers to basic genealogical questions by mail, but the vast majority are understaffed and have neither the time or inclination to reply. A positive response is not to be taken for granted as the limitations of research by mail should be explicit. On the spot research for anything more than the most general questions is always recommended, although it is understood that the vast majority of American genealogists will be unable to accomplish this during their lifetime. It is then recommended that a competent area researcher be engaged to do the work.

Desired archival material can be located by consulting a card catalog if one visits the facility in person. If this personal contact is not possible, one can become familiar with an archival collection by studying the contents of a published catalog, inventory, or descriptive guide, if one has been published.

Many things can be learned by carefully reading the inventories. Among them are: the name and address of the main office; name and status of the person(s) designated in-charge and his or her assistants; business hours; mission statement; scope (jurisidiction) and profile of the collection; restrictions on the use of the records and admission requirements, if any exist; how requests for information or research are dealt with by personnel; library loan facilities (especially to overseas libraries); the ability to determine if an archive's stacks are open or closed; number of reading rooms open to the public; photocopying facilities and charges; bibliography of previously published articles, books, catalogues, guides and inventories about the archives; dates of the earliest records held by the archive of genealogical and historical value; and major types of genealogical records available. The total number of volumes, manuscripts, maps, and periodicals. Emphasis is commonly placed on special collections. The capacity and rate of accessions of a repository can be ascertained. Sometimes a little background information on the creation of the archives is given together with a sketch of the buildings in which the collections are housed.

A substantial number of archive inventories can be found under various subject headings in US libraries (especially in university libraries). They may be located under "Archives", "Historical Sources", or "Inventories" among other categories. They may also be purchased, if still in print, from the archive for a reasonable price. Out-of-print volumes may be photocopied, in part or in whole, when available. They are, of course, written in German, for the most part. Some get more specific in detail than others. While some progress from topics of general interest, others list specific documents and list the names of persons from emigration papers, citizenship certificates, etc.

So individuals do not spend an inordinate amount of time searching for an inventory of the archive they are interested in, it may be suggested that consultation with one of the works containing a large number of entries be used. Three compendium sources are available for purchase from German book dealers or are in US libraries: One source is the MINERVA-HANDBUECHER ARCHIVE: ARCHIVE IM DEUTSCHSPRACHIGEN RAUM, 2nd edition, Berlin and New York, 1974. 1418 pages, 2 volumes. ISBN 3-11-001955-8. This important reference work contains entries for archives in West Germany (F.R.G.), the German Democratic Republic, Austria and Switzerland. Another work, ARCHIVE UND ARCHIVARE IN DER BUNDESREPUBLIK DEUTSCHLAND, OESTERREICH UND DER SCHWEIZ. 14th edition, 1985-1986, Munich, 1986. 231 pages, a relatively up-to-date compilation featuring approximately 1500 entries of archives in the FRG, Austria and Switzerland. The third is, VERZEICHNISSE DER ARCHIVARE, published by Verlag Degener & Co. (D-8530) Neustadt an der Aisch, 1975.

Since inventorying any collection is an enormous task, printed catalogues may have a limited scope, and can cover only a short span of years. Their production may be limited also, as they are not compiled at any specific intervals and are not frequently updated.

PRIMARY SOURCES 19TH-17TH CENTURY

PRIMARY SOURCES — 19th CENTURY

Emigration Records

Since it was the official policy of the German states to prohibit emigration until the beginning of the 19th century, one cannot expect to find a substantial amount of documentation on the people departing before that time. Records of emigration and immigration are mainly a 19th century phenomena.

Most often, in the past, population or group migrations were studied and recorded without regard to the individuals involved. When officials began recording emigrations, the early lists usually enumerated the names of the organizers and male members of the party. Little information of genealogical value is included in early emigration lists. Two major academic areas, sociology and demography, in which researchers have concentrated their studies on migrations, have served to document and preserve data about the movements, causes, and numbers of individuals.

It wasn't until the middle of the 19th century when records of individual emigrants began to appear regularily. Since emigration was officially prohibited by the German states in the 18th century, we can not expect to find records kept by local administrators. In so far as record keeping is concerned, mobility has proved to be a curse to genealogists for generations since it makes finding the place of origin harder.

Despite restrictions placed on the emigrants by their governments, several thousand people left Germany during the 18th century for places like Russia, Eastern Europe and North America. There are, however, few records containing enough information to identify individuals making the journeys during this period. Early lists enumerated, at best, the group leaders and other male members of the parties, but little information of genealogical value was added. Many of the 18th century lists have been published and can be accessed in archives and libraries.

Keeping records of emigrants and their families was primarily the responsibility of local village or city authorities. In some cases, ministers also particpated by adding the time of departure into the parish register. Notations such as "the family has emigrated" or simply, "to

America" have been found in records of the church. The frequency, quality and content of the documentation on emigration varies parish to parish.

If the law was followed, a formal request for permission to emigrate was submitted to a local magistrate. He identified the intended emigrants, listed their occupations, date and place of birth, marriage date, parent's names, spouse's name, birth date of spouse, parents of spouse, names of children, date of birth for the children and the final destination, if known. The original list or a transcipt thereof was generally forwarded to a higher district or regional official, making it possible to find such documentation in both municipal and regional archives. Papers also produced in the process might be applications for release of citizenship, passport applications, etc. Names of military service dodgers, deserters, announcements in newspapers of those who didn't give up their citizenship, and persons declared legally dead by heirs. For a more detailed description of these and other records created by the emigration process (the so-called emigration literature), and a narrative about the European ports of departure and passenger lists, see Wellauer's, GERMAN IMMIGRATION TO AMERICA IN THE NINETEENTH CENTURY: A GENEALOGIST'S GUIDE, Milwaukee, 1985.

German emigrants mostly used non-German ports until the end of the 1830's. The early ports chosen were located in Holland, Belgium and France. The Northern German port cities of Bremen and Hamburg attracted the emigrant trade at the beginning of the 1830's. Unfortunately, Bremen's port lists, which began as early as 1832, were destroyed at the end of the century, however, the lists of the port of Hamburg are extant from 1850. The lists of departing German emigrants (Passagierlisten) are deposited in various locations. For addresses (see Appendix D)

Civil Registration (Personenstandregister)

The body of records which genealogists rely upon most often are those primary sources which contain vital statistics. Important information provided in records of the church are baptisms, marriages, and burials. The act of recording vital statistics by secular authorities was referred to as civil registration. While civil records contain documentation of births, marriages, and deaths occurring within an area called a civil district, it was the duty of the religious authorities to record events of importance to the church, that is, the baptism, marriage and burials occurring within a congregation.

Civil record keeping became mandatory in Prussia in October 1874 to January 1876 in other areas of the German Empire, as a result of its recent unification. Earlier civil registers were kept in areas west of the Rhine River. Depending upon the location of a region, civil registration began at intervals. The following list should indicate the approximate beginnings in German areas:

a) Alsace (Elsass) c. 1798
   -includes the following areas, which are located today in France: Strasbourg in the Lower Rhine district (Bas-Rhin) and Colmar in the Upper Rhine district (Haut-Rhin)

b) Anhalt-1850
   -today Anhalt is divided between Magdeburg and Halle, areas part of the German Democratic Republic (East Germany)

c) Baden, c. 1798
   -includes the areas of Baden-Baden and Baden-Durlach

d) Bavaria (Bayern)-1876

e) Brandenburg-1874

f) Bremen-1866
   -one of the Hanseatic Free Cities

g) Brunswick- (Braunschweig)-1876

h) Hamburg-1809
   -one of the Hanseatic Free Cities

i) Hannover (Hanover)-1809
   -Hannover occupies much of what is known as Lower Saxony today. In 1866, Hannover became part of Prussia

j) Hesse (Hessen)-1803
   -formerly Hessen was divided into two principalities, Hesse-Darmstadt (Hessen-Darmstadt) and Hesse-Cassel (Hessen-Kassel)

k)   Hesse-Nassau (Hessen-Nassau)-1803
        -at the time Hesse-Cassel was annexed to
Prussia (1866) the name was changed to Hesse-Nassau

l)   Lippe-1876
     -today Lippe is part of North Rhein-Westphalia
(Nordrhein-Westfalen)

m)   Lorraine (Lothringen) c.1798

n)   Luebeck-1803

o)   Mecklenburg-1876
            -part of the German Democratic Republic
today. Includes the districts of Potsdam, Rostock
and Schwerin

p)   Oldenburg-1811

q)   Palatinate (Pfalz) c.1798

r)   Pomerania (Pommern)-1874

s)   Prussia-(Preussen)-1874
     -the Kingdom of Prussia includes Brandenburg,
East Prussia (Ostpreussen) Pomerania (Pommern),
Posen, Silesia (Schlesien), Schleswig-Holstein and
West Prussia (Westpreussen)

t)   Rhine Province (Rhineland) (Rheinprovinz)-
c.1798
        -made part of Prussia in 1815

u)   Saxony -1876

v)   Schleswig-Holstein -1874

w)   Silesia (Schlesien) -1874

x)   Thuringia (Thueringia)- 1876

y)   Westphalia (Westfalen)- 1808

z)   Wuerttemburg- 1876

        Presently, civil records are still kept, for
the most part, in local repositories. A local
repository (Standesamt) may include one or more
villages in its area of jurisdiction, depending on
the size of the population. You must know the exact
commune to which you should address any questions
about a civil record.

For each photocopy or abstract requested, expect to be charged a small fee. Service and copy fees vary from place to place, so before sending money to cover expenses and labor, it is best to wait to be billed. Many civil records have been microfilmed by the GS. Some have been indexed or have been placed in the International Genealogical Index (IGI) as a result of the controlled extraction program conducted in recent years.

The creation of civil records occurred in many areas similtaneously with parish registers. This created a dual system of registration of vital events of the past 100 years or more.

Records of the Church

The parish registers (Kirchenbuecher) are THE major source of genealogical data, a primary source record dating back to the earliest books kept at the end of the 15th century. They have received the most attention in literature on German genealogical source material, mainly because they make up the bulk of most accessible collections in archives in the United States and Europe.

German Protestants began record-keeping before the Catholics did. The first Protestant books were kept in Baden around 1531. Other areas in Germany, such as Saxony, have Protestant records dating back to 1540. The registers of Stuttgart date back to 1558 and can be found in print. Other published records include those of Calw, Esslingen, Ludwigsburg, and Tuebingen. Although many of the parishes in Wuerttemberg have books extant from the mid-sixteenth century, some of these registers have gaps, are incomplete or damaged.

Catholic parishes in Europe were mandated to begin keeping registers by an edict from the Council of Trent (1563), but most did not begin the task until after 1600. Even then, some survived only a short time. The vast devastation of the Thirty Years War (1618-1648) caused the loss or damage of a great number of registers, particularily in the area known as the Palatinate.

In general, widespread record-keeping in parishes did not occur until after the Reformation, when it became important to declare one's affiliation. Records of the Reformed churches began around 1650.

The principal portions of the church register are the baptisms, marriages and burial records. Our attention will be directed to these sections, while additional comments concerning the remarkable contents of some minor parts will be discussed. Each faith kept the specific portions according to their own rules, therefore there will be some variation between a Catholic burial citation and one found in a Protestant or Evangelical church, for instance.

Baptismal Register (Taufregister)

Of the three major portions of a parish register, the baptismal record is usually the most extensive and continuous. Live births, as well as a number of stillborn babies (some labeled as such even though they may have lived a few days following birth), were recorded. Because of a high rate of infant mortality in previous centuries, many children didn't survive long enough to be confirmed or to marry. For this reason, those who died young may appear in a register only once in their lifetime. In fact, if a child died at a young age, the notation of the date of death is sometimes written as a part of the baptismal entry. A cross beside the date of baptism is not uncommon to indicate the death of that person.

Before the 19th century, it is unusual to find a register in a pre-printed form, therefore, it is difficult to predict a continuity of style. The styles of parish registers vary from region to region. They often contain common elements like the date of baptism (sometimes also the date of birth), the child's Christian and surname, parent's names, and names of sponsors or godparents. Occasionally, the day and time of birth are given also.

Beware of transcriptions or abstractions from original ledgers. It is always preferable to use the primary rather than the secondary source, when available.

It is not uncommon to find that grandparents, aunts or uncles were chosen as godparents, thereby making it possible to establish relationships between the child and the sponsors.

Marriage Register (Trauregister) (Eheregister)

The marriage record is possibly the most complete of the major sections and therefore genealogically the most valuable. Ordinarily, entries contain the full name of the bridegroom and bride, date of marriage, occupation of the groom, place of residence for both and the location of the ceremony. The marriage entry will most likely be found in the bride's church (her home parish), if her place of residence is different from that of the groom.

Rules were sometimes flagrented within the church to suit the times. Marriages outside of consangunity were forbidden, or defined according to the laws of the times. Marriages were also contracted to increase territory, impose sovereignty and to join in alliances. In related events, such as divorce, rules of the church often permitted or recalled as grounds for divorce. Children could be legitimized by decree, not only through matrimony.

Burial Register (Grabnisregister)

Death registers, particularily the earliest volumes, are poor for genealogical purposes when compared to the baptism or marriage registers. The contents of a typical entry contains the date of burial (sometimes, but not always, accompanied by the date of death), the name of the deceased and the cause of death. Usually the deceased is identified as "the wife of", or "the son of", but if no identifying characteristics were given, it is difficult to prove a relationship. To make a positive identification, some mention of occupation, parentage, spouse, age, birthplace or birthdate is necessary. The latter is often miscalculated because of the uncertainty of the actual birthdate. This is especially true in areas where the death occurred shortly after the baptismal records were created or if the deceased was buried in a district other than where he was born.

Depending on the size of the congregation(s) under the jurisdiction of a particular minister, the baptisms, marriages and burials may be found in one or more volumes. They may be bound into a single book, arranged chronologically or kept in separate volumes. In guidebooks to German records, little emphasis has been placed on educating the readers on the use of additional church records, kept in addition to the sacraments. These "minor" records include:

a)   Ministerial Lists- a roster of those who
served the parish from the establishment of the
parish record. This might include the names of past
ministers, their places of origin with a commentary
on their preparations for the job.

b)   betrothals (engagement announcements)

c)   marriage banns

        -a couple was required to register their
intent to marry. The proposed union was announced
several times in the church before the actual
ceremony took place. It is possible that a couple
never participated in a formal marriage ceremony
after their names appeared in the banns.

d)   confirmation (Konfirmanden) lists

        -coverage ranges from simply the number of
those confirmed to entries containing the
confirmant's name, residence, father's name, and
date of birth. For young persons between the ages
of 14 and 19, mainly.

e)   communion - usually only names given. Other
identifying data is lacking in this record.

f)   membership lists (MitgleiderListen)

        -occasionally kept to record movements in
and out of the parish or to record contributions.
May also appear as a list of souls
(Seelenregister), which is an official parish
census.

g)   records of the poor- mission lists

h)   pew tax lists- a "reservation" of sorts for a
couple or family. Men and women were often
separated in the pews in many churches.

i)   bell tax (bell toll) (Jahrzeitbuecher)

        -small amount paid by members of the
deceased's family to ring the church bell three to
four days following the date of burial.

j)   shroud tax

        -small amount paid by the deceased's family
to wrap a body in a burial cloth. Both the bell
and shroud taxes can be used to document the burial
date of a person in the absence of a burial

register or death record. Relationship to the deceased can be gleaned by noting who paid the taxes.

k)   vaccination records

        -occurring in the provinces of Schleswig and Holstein particularily. Many emigrants carried their vaccination documents to America with them.

l)   family register (Familienregister)

        -contains vital statistics of a whole family, arranged somewhat in the same form as a modern day family group chart. The registers were kept since the beginning of the 17th century, mostly by Catholics, but can also be found in Protestant parishes. Much time can be saved by tracing a lineage through a family register, since relationships have already been determined.

        Keep in mind that a margin of error can be calculated into all of these records. If the family register was reconstructed after the members of a family were deceased, relationships were sometimes assumed. Names of dead children may have been omitted from family groups if the record was created after the fact. Servants and other live-ins might be included in a household. When a person died and left the parish, the minister often crossed off the name, making the entry difficult to decifer. The baptisms, marriages and burials were most likely the source of information used when compiling the family register and mistakes were frequently made in the transcription. It is therefore best to consult the parish register for the original entries.

        Laws of years gone by in the German states allowed royalty, nobility (estate holders), and the military to keep separate parish registers. Therefore, we can expect to find, in some cases, the records of the baptisms, marriages and burials of unlanded peasants residing on estates recorded in special registers. Men in the military may have had their children baptized in a garrison church instead of in their "home" parish. When the marriages of officers occurred they were also entered in such registers. A number of Prussian military or regimental parish registers (Militaer Kirchenbuecher) have been microfilmed by the Genealogical Society of Utah (LDS).

In order to become familiar with the potential value of a parish register, a researcher must be prepared to do more than search for individual names and dates. To discover hidden clues, one must pay close attention to the general composition of this source. A person's economic status, legitimacy, religion, social standing, occupation and relationship to others may be reconstructed by utilizing the inferences. For instance, the social standing of a couple may be inferred by reading the names of the sponsors. Rarely were the sponsors at a baptism chosen from a higher social class than that to which the parents belonged. If a noble couple chose peasants as sponsors, the birth could have been illegimate.

The economic status of church members might not be apparent until handwriting patterns displayed throughout a register are studied. A person of wealth may have had the baptism of a child recorded in letters larger than those used to record other baptisms. The variations noted in several volumes may have been up to two inches in height.

Illegitimate births were appended virtually all the time with the German terms "uneheliches Kind" or the abbreviation "unehel." or with the Latin term, "spurius", or "spuria" or the abbreviation, "spur." A variety of other techniques were used when a minister wished to call attention to a noteable birth. One pastor wrote his illegitimate baptisms upside down so the volume would have to be up-ended to read them. Another used his worst handwriting on one parent entries.

Rarely did a marriage occur between two persons of different confessions, i.e. a Catholic man and a Protestant woman, for instance. When a ceremony of this type was performed, it was after one of the couple converted to the religion of the church in which they were married.

It is possible to make contact with a parish directly, and is frequently done by addressing an airmail envelope in the following manner:

For Protestant churches:

Evangelische Pfarramt
D- _____ (4 digit postal code here + town name)

For Catholic churches:

        Katholisches Pfarramt
        D-_____ (4 digit postal code here + town name)

        Before writing to a parish, make a careful
search of US archives and libraries to be sure you
are unable to to the same work in the United
States.

        Type, or neatly print, your request on a white
sheet of paper. If you are not fluent in German, do
not put forth a half-hearted effort with the
language. You may write in English, if this is the
language with which you can best express yourself.
The reply will be sent in German, most likely, the
language of their best ability. Enclose three
International Reply coupons for return postage.
After the coupons are exchanged at a foreign post
office for stamps, two are no longer sufficient to
cover the cost of a return airmail letter. A
self-addressed envelope should not be included
since it weighs down the letter and the receiver
will most likely use one of his own stationery.

        Funeral Sermons (Leichenpredigten)

        Funeral sermons or memorial speeches, were
Protestant records, created after the Reformation,
lasting until about the middle of the 18th century.

        They will be found for families belonging to
the higher economic stratum. About two-thirds of
them pertain to men, the other third to women and
children. Each ranges from one to 300 pages in
length and contain the family name, given name,
life span, birthplace and profesion, plus notable
events occurring in the life of the deceased,
sometimes compiled by the deceased themselves.

Minority Religious Records

Minority religious groups flourished in Germany in past centuries. Before the 19th century, membership in churches other than Protestant, Catholic or Reformed accounted for only a small portion of the total population. They included Baptists, Huguenot, Jewish, Mennonite, and Methodist, among others.

Jewish Records

Persons with German-Jewish heritage have special problems tracing their origins beyond the 19th century. There were some reasons why record-keeping was not begun earlier in Jewish communities. First, nothing in Jewish law mandated keeping records. Secondly, family names were frequently changed or there were none at all. Thirdly, there was no practical advantage in keeping registers. Jewish communities were generally small in the 17th and 18th centuries and they maintained strong oral traditions.

Jewish registers began to appear in Germany in the 18th century. One type of register kept in Jewish communities were circumcision records (they serve as registration of birth, since the ceremony took place eight days later); marriage records and burial records.

When Jewish people were integrated into German communities, local administrations incooperated them into their civil registrations during the latter part of the 18th and 19th centuries. The Prussian government ordered Jewish families to establish family names and registered them accordingly. Jews were included in tax levying rolls and in population censuses in some areas.

In a few areas, communities granted Jews citizenship rights. In the community of Muehlhausen, for example, seventeen documents concerning the "Buergerrecht der Juden, 1800-1868", exist in the archives there.

The records of some Jewish congregations located in the eastern provinces, including East Prussia, West Prussia, Pomerania, Lower and Upper Silesia, are centralized at: Bundesarchiv, Am Woellershof 12, D-5400 Koblenz, Federal Republic of Germany. The archive of the Jewish community in Berlin is located at Fasanenstrasse 79, D-1000 Berlin 12.

A listing of Jewish congregational records which have been microfilmed by the Genealogical Society (LDS) was published a few years ago in the periodical, TOLEDOT. This organization has been instrumental in identifying source material of genealogical value. Toledot may be contacted at 155 East 93 Street, Suite 3C, New York, New York, 10028. Two other U.S. based organizations with archives on German and Eastern European Jewry include the Leo Baeck Institute, 129 East 73 St. New York, New York, 10021 and the YIVO Institute for Jewish Research, 1048 Fifth Ave. New York, New York, 10028. The latter's collection reflects an emphasis on the areas of Baden, Berlin, Northern Germany, the Palatinate and West Prussia. There are deposited a substantial number of circumcision records for Northern German areas such as Schleswig-Holstein and Frankfurt a. M. and death records from the eastern provinces.

The records of other German Jews may also be located in Israel at the Central Archive for the History of the Jewish People (P.O. Box 1026, Jerusalem). This location is considered to be a worldwide historical repository for Jewish records. Their holdings include records of German towns with Jewish inhabitants.

Civil registration of births, marriages and deaths were kept by municipal authorities. Only a few of these early records of Jewish origin survived the period before and during World War II. If a Jewish family intergrated into a German commune in the 19th century, one may find evidence left in an area's civil records where they were recorded, together with other citizens, regardless of their religious affiliations. TOLEDOT published a list of microfilm numbers of the civil registration records for Jewish communities in Germany in the Summer 1978 issue, Vol. 2, No. 1.

If civil records are non-extant, records of population movements (Melderegister) also appeared in the 19th century and can be used in lieu of the destruction of civil records. Citizenship records, passports, and passenger lists, have for the most part, been helpful in the search for Jewish ancestry.

The address of the central archive of German Jewry is: Gesamtarchiv der deutschen Juden, D-1000 Berlin 15, Joachimstalerstrasse 13, FRG.

One valuable source, compiled mainly by survivors of various Eastern European communities following World War II, are the "Yizkor" books or memorial books. Each volume contains a history of the commune, with profiles of families from the district, lists of those who perished during the war, and so forth. The "Zizkor" books are kept in libraries and research institutions with special collection on the Jewish people, located in New York and California.

Mennonite Records

Lists of Mennonites, periodically checked by authorities in the 16th and 17th centuries who sought to persecute the membership, were discontinued in later years. For this reason, other record forms we must rely on are extant tax, probate and land registers. Since this group is known for the careful recording of land transactions, this record, in some cases, may make up for the lack of vital records, due to its richness of genealogical material.

Some Mennonite couples went to Lutheran ministers to be married. Records of Mennonites ofttimes were preserved within the pages of a local Protestant or Catholic parish.

The Mennonite Research Center, (Archiv des Mennonitischen Geschichtsvereins), D-6719 Weierhof bei Marnheim, Federal Republic of Germany, may be consulted for further assistance.

Census Records

Census records, or more literally, population counts, were not taken, in the German states, on a regular dicennial basis as in the United States. Any list which enumerates the local inhabitants can be referred to as a "census". Early tax rolls can be used as an identification tool because they usually included the names of the heads of families.

The so-called census records go by a variety of German names, such as Bevoelkerungslisten, Einwohnerslisten and Volkszahlungungslisten. In the 1700's, some areas created censuses containing the names of landowners, or oaths of allegiances. Some governments made lists of emigrants and "absent" persons (or emigrants). In 1744, in Wuerttemberg, a census was made containing approximately 100,000 names. Church visitations, tax lists, and Stadtbuecher from Pomerania provide the earliest documentation of the resident populations in that region.

Good family information was also collected in Schleswig-Holstein through census records when they were taken with some regularity. They were, however, interrupted frequently in the 19th century by wars and occupations.

Military Records (Musterungslisten)

Although most young men served in the militia some time during their residence in Germany, military do not constitute a major genealogical source in the Federal Republic of Germany.

The main reason for this is the fact that various types of military papers are scattered in a number of archives located throughout Germany. At best, if an ancestor's unit or regiment can be identified, documentation may be found only after a considerable amount of effort. Many works have previously been published identifying the Hessian mercenary soldiers, engaged by the British to fight in the American Revolutionary War against the colonists. (see HETRINA and various titles by Clifford Neal Smith). More recently, lists of casualties of the Seven Weeks' War (1866) and the Franco-Prussian War (1870-1871) have been released (Wellauer, GERMAN CASUALTIES OF THE SEVEN WEEKS' WAR (1866) AND THE FRANCO-PRUSSIAN WAR (1870-1871), Milwaukee, 1986 and PRUSSIAN AND SAXON CASUALTIES OF THE FRANCO-PRUSSIAN WAR (1870-1871)

Under the heading of military records, we find muster rolls, regimental histories, pension records, lists of deserters, lists of officers (Ranglisten), dating from c. 1780, and lists of intentions to emigrate. Together, they yield a complete picture of the soldiers, including the birthdate and place, rank, unit, regiment, commanding officer's name, action (battles), awards, appointments, promotions, deeds of valor, wounds, deathdate and place.

(For addresses, see Appendix E)

TRACING A PEDIGREE BEFORE THE 16TH CENTURY

Some German pedigrees can be extended to the 17th century by following the methodology prescribed in previous sections, provided that the general condition and availability of the records of a particular area are good. If they are not, it becomes increasingly more difficult to continue before the 1600's.

Researchers may encounter major pitfalls in their endeavours caused by a combination of social, political, religious and economic factors of medieval times. It is therefore advisable to know what to look for and what to watch out for in early records. It is important to keep in mind that the history of the 14th-16th centuries was virtually constructed from genealogies of nobility; tracing dynastic lines and family connections, infused by the idea of the noble's being superior. The lives of commoners and women, in particular, were rarely documented or recorded, but literature on noble families was prolific.

The French Revolution reversed this trend of "over documenting" the nobles in Europe. Afterward, historians came to view the common man as a hero and portrayed the noblemen and kings as monsters.

The first records of common persons were included in census returns, tax lists, visitations and military rolls. These records did not begin until the 17th century in most areas and then they often included only household heads and male children. The beginning of the 16th century marked a great interest in record-keeping.

In the German states, it was most often the landowners, clergy, nobility, and royalty who had genealogies compiled for them. Common in lineages traced to 1500 was the claim of descent from a family of the ancient Roman Empire. Because it was the fashionable thing to do, many early genealogists supplemented their work by filling in charts with ancient noble orders. Many male connections in 15th century royal or noble families are suspect. Since genealogies of nobles include dates, not places, they are difficult to prove. The nobility were very mobile, which complicated the record-keeping.

Early noblemen were known to have taken more than one wife on occasion. Problems resulted when the children of these unions were traced. Some children of a second marriage received a medium rank of nobility, while others were bestowed with full titles. Illegitimate offspring were sometimes legitimized by a strong union. These illegitimate children could inherit a title of higher nobility, but rarely one of lower rank. These practices (or customs) complicated the line of heredity.

In response to the Reformation, which occurred in the middle of the 16th century, a number of Protestant families voluntarily gave up titles granted to them by Roman Catholic monarchs in reformed areas. Traces of the titles have diminished throughout subsequent generations. Bitter rivalries during this time split families and caused liasons. It was not uncommon to discover Catholic families being driven from strong reformed territories and changing locations.

During the Middle Ages, religion controlled lives and laws. Dispensations were sought and purchased for legitimizing children, for burials, marriages and for trade. It may be difficult to project ourselves into the moral and emotional structure of that time using today's values and mores. Confusion by date references prior to the calendar change compounded problems. Many events were dated by a religious calendar, for example. A baptism may have been reported as occurring two days after the Nativity of the Virgin or a Monday after Epiphany. Sometimes the year began with dating in a papal year or from the reigning King's accession. For this reason, medieval chronology is hard to document. If a year was considered to begin at Easter, this could be anywhere from March 22 to April 22, but usually March 25 was preferred. The New Style calender took over in the 16th century, but it was not accepted everywhere until the 18th century. The new calender was accepted in Catholic areas before Protestant.

The period between 800 and 1500 is characterized by periods of plagues, wars, bad government, schism in the church, social unrest, economic chaos and depraved morals, together with social and religious hysteria. It was described as a bad time, with few, and poor records being kept. Accuracy and verification are difficult to find in records before 1500. Facts were supposed to be recorded in manuscript sources or transmitted orally. Variations in names and record keeping make details hard to distinguish. Even estimates of seemingly significant data such as an entire country's population may vary from 21 million to 10 million. The tendency to exaggerate numbers or round them off was commonplace. Questioning the accuracy of figures of this sort certainly affects the study and evaluation of other related data, especially that of genealogical pursuits. What makes the task doubly trying is that it was often hard to distinguish the same person from source to source. Personal descriptions were sometimes contradictory at best. A man described in one source as short and dark, for example, may be portrayed in another as tall and blonde. One source may identify a man by his Christian name, Hanns, while another, he may be simply counted as "the Baker" in another paper.

Pre-dating Parish Registers

In early records, pre-dating parish registers, the emphasis was most frequently placed on the negative happenings. That is, the survival of the "bad side of humanity". Early documents include information about lawsuits, criminal acts, court actions, misbehaviors, and crises such as fires, wars, famines and plagues. History and genealogy must be formulated from surviving documents.

Many genealogies have been extended beyond the 16th century by researchers who have sufficed for generations by using nebulous terminology and dubious technique, for example, assigning relationships or permanence by using "presumably" or "probably" the "son of" or the" tenant of". Many pedigrees extended in this manner have added 200 or 300 years after concrete evidence and source material have been exhausted. It would be noteworthy to remember the story of one town chronicler, an early family historian of his time, who encountered great difficulty in tracing his own pedigree back to 1499 without breaks. He observed this while engaging in the task in 1753, that even though a legend indicated that the family originated in the town since 1240, the available data was insufficient to support any legitimate claims.

Some cautions should be observed when relying on the parish register as the only source of genealogical data. First, a lineage traced through parish registers only is incomplete, i.e. unsubstantiated. One source may be used as evidence, but rarely can one piece of evidence prove a lineage beyond a reasonable doubt. As much supporting data as possible must be accumulated.

Second, since parish registers have a cut-off date, a lineage would inevitably end when the parish registers cease to exist if other sources are not sought.

Thirdly, natural destruction and assorted catastrophes have affected the availability of parish registers. The occurances of wars, fires, etc. have caused the destruction or damaged to parts or whole registers. Some registers were not started until the early 19th century. To reconstruct a damaged entry, auxiliary sources of the same period must be located.

Fourth, ecclesiastical records were kept in a variety of ways. Lack of direction or continuity is a contributing factor. Secular authorities may have influenced how vital statistics were recorded. Historical events like famine and sickness affected the tone and substance of the record.

Fifth, when a primary source becomes a secondary source, errors in transcription may be assumed. Unless the original copy of a register has been destroyed, all attempts should be made to consult the original copy.

Finally, parish registers supply relatively little information on individual lives. At best, a variety of deductive and inductive reasoning skills must be employed to make the most of the available source material.

Frequently, lineage work is discontinued when one is unaware of the (LIFE BEFORE PARISH REGISTERS). Since the recognition of limitations in the use of parish registers as a major source of genealogical data, an effort has been made to identify alternative sources. A variety of miscellaneous material allows extraordinary opportunities to compare evidence found in parish registers or civil records, or to continue reconstruction of a family history into the period pre-dating their creation.

In total, this documentation is referenced as "minor sources", because their appearance is irregular or atypical. This includes non-parochial records created selectively and are, in many cases, scarce, and obscure. Most remain unpublished, unindexed and exist in manuscript form. This group accounts for a very small percentage of the total documentation created in previous centuries. This source material can be found in provincial and municipal archives in the area of search. Research in person is recommended to examine these records.

Often, at least one hundred years can be added beyond the point when parish registers began by using a body of extant probate files. The major documents contained in this source are the wills or (Testamente), which began to appear around the beginning of the 13th century. Living family members and heirs can be listed, in addition to their places of residence, occupations and other details of genealogical value. Sometimes if a member of the family was purposely disinherited, the reasons for the action were recorded in even greater detail. A complete enumeration of personal and real property are generally included with the will plus a statement(s) of disposition. Of particular interest is the fact that the deceased's signature appears on the document.

A vast majority of the records which pre-date parish registers have something to do with land or taxes. Many regional and local archives have documents pertaining to portions of land in their jurisdictions which date back to the 8th and 9th centuries. The records of the conveyances, rental agreements, etc. constitute a body of land records referred to as Grundbuecher. The emphasis is more on the description of the land rather than on individuals or families, but often relationships are recognizable throughout these land records. For example, a man may be leasing a piece of land with his brothers (who are then also named), who are then identified as the sons of a woman in the town, who is the widow of the local barber. Economic status can also be found or inferred by the amounts posted during the transaction.

A checklist of early sources created between the 14th to 19th centuries, available from the repositories listed herein, might be helpful:

_____hospital records (Spital)

_____construction records, including registrations of house numbers, house markings, etc.

_____transactions, indebtedness letters (Kauf- und Schuldbriefe)

_____rent (Rentenbuecher) (income)

_____hunting rights (Jagdrecht)

_____water rights (Wasserleitungen)

_____fishing rights (Fischerei)

_____forest rights (wood tax) (Rechnungen des Forstamtes)

_____fire protection

_____farm taxes (on wagons, horses, rooms, etc.)

_____poor house records (Armenhaus)

_____court records, (Gerichtsprotokolle) (Amtsgerichter) including probate, guardianship, inheritance, etc.

_____guild records (Zunftbuecher)(Meisterrecht) (Gefaelle) (includes occupational,unions,apprentice certificates)

_____newspapers (Zeitungen)

_____city chronicles (Stadtchroniken) (Aktensammlungen) (Formularbuecher)

_____estate (probate) records (Testemente) (Hinterlassende)

_____city directories (Adressbuecher)

_____funeral sermons (Leichenpredigten)

_____welfare (c.18-19th centuries)

_____university lists (Universitaetsmatrikeln)

_____school gymnasium, c.1800 (Schulmatrikeln)

_____police (PolizeiRegister) (includes a rich variety of criminal cases, cause of death unknown, murders, and even animals checks)

_____military records (Musterungslisten)

_____tax rolls (Steuerbuecher)

_____land records (Grundbuecher)

_____citizen registers (Buergerbuecher) (Buerger-Gemeinderoedel)

_____parish registers (Kirchenbuecher)

_____census   (Volkszahlungslisten)
(Bevoelkerungslisten)

_____birth and marriage letters   (Geburts-u.
Hochzeits Briefe)

Conclusion

There are a large number of archives located
in West Germany which collectively contain a
substantial body of documentation of potential
value to genealogists. It is the main
responsibility of researchers to make every effort
to familiarize themselves with them.

In order to trace a lineage through German
records and to realize the full potential of the
information contained in the sources, a working
knowledge of the material is necessary. More than a
passing effort is needed to become a well-informed
genealogist, since the distance between the source
and the researcher is usually considerable.

Genealogy involves more than using parish
registers as the primary source of data. Many other
comtemporary records, some pre-dating the 16h
century, should be utilized to produce a complete
family study. Effective methodology includes the
close scrutiny of extant primary and secondary
sources.

APPENDICES

Appendix A

STATE ARCHIVES IN THE FEDERAL REPUBLIC OF GERMANY

For the upper Palatinate:
Staatsarchiv fuer Oberpfalz
D-8450 Amberg
Archivstrasse 3

For east Frisia:
Staatsarchiv fuer Ostfriesland
D-2960 Aurich
Georg strasse 50

For Upper Franconia:
Staatsarchiv fuer Oberfranken
D-8600 Bamberg
Hainstrasse 39
Postfach 2668

For the city of West Berlin:
Landesarchiv Berlin
D-1000 Berlin 12
Strasse des 17 Juni. 112

For the city of Berlin:
Geheimes Staatsarchiv
D-1000 Berlin 33 (Dahlem)
Archivstrasse 12-14

For the city of Bremen:
Staatsarchiv
D-2800 Bremen
Praesident-Kennedy-Platz 2

For the Rhineland:
Personenstandsarchiv Bruehl
D-5040 Bruehl
Schlossstrasse 12

For Lower Saxony, Schaumburg-Lippe:
Niedersaechisches Staatsarchiv
D-4967 Bueckeburg
Schloss

Staatsarchiv fuer Coburg
D-8630 Coburg
Schloss Ehrenburg

For Hesse-Darmstadt:
Staatarchiv fuer Hessen-Darmstadt
D-6100 Darmstadt
Schloss

For Lippe and Westphalia:
Staatsarchiv
D-4930 Detmold
Willi-Hofmannstrasse 2

For the Rhineland, Nordrhein-Westfalen:
Hauptstaatsarchiv
D-4000 Duesseldorf
Prinz-Georgstrasse 78

For Baden:
Badisches Generallandesarchiv
D-7800 Freiburg
Colombistrasse 4

For the city of Hamburg:
Staatsarchiv
D-2000 Hamburg
Rathaus ABCstrasse 19

For Lower Saxony:
Staatsarchiv fuer Hannover
D-3000 Hannover
Am Archiv 1

For Baden:
Generallandesarchiv
D-7500 Karlsruhe
Noerdliche Hilda-Promenade 2

For the north Palatinate-Rhineland:
Staatsarchiv
Karmeliterstrasse 1-3
D-5400 Koblenz

For Lower Bavaria:
Staatsarchiv fuer Niederbayern
D-8300 Landshut
Burg Trausnitz

For Wuerttemberg:
Staatsarchiv
Schloss
D-7140 Ludwigsburg

For Schleswig-Holstein:
Staatsarchiv Luebeck
D-2400 Luebeck
Sankt Annenstrasse 2

For Hesse-Cassel:
Staatsarchiv fuer Hessen-Kassel
D-3550 Marburg a. Lahn
Friedrichsplatz 15

For Bavaria, southern Germany:
Hauptstaatsarchiv
D-8000 Muenchen 2
Arcisstrasse 12

For Upper Bavaria:
Staatsarchiv fuer Oberbayern
D-8000 Muenchen
Schoenfeldstrasse 3

Staatsarchiv
D-4400 Muenster
Bohlweg 2

For Swabia:
Staatsarchiv fuer Schwaben
D-8858 Neuburg a.d. Donau
Schloss

For Middle Franconia:
Staatsarchiv fuer Mittelfranken
D-8500 Nuernberg
Archivstrasse 17

For Lower Saxony:
Staatsarchiv fuer Oldenburg
D-2900 Oldenburg
Damm 43

For Lower Saxony:
Staatsarchiv fuer Osnabrueck
D-4500 Osnabrueck
Schlossstrasse 29

For the Saarland:
Landesarchiv
D-6600 Saarbruecken
Scheidterstrasse 114

For Schleswig-Holstein:
Landesarchiv
D-2380 Schleswig
Schloss Gottorf

For the Rhineland:
Staatsarchiv
D-4000 Schloss Kalkum
Zweigstelle Kalkum

For Wuerttemberg:
Staatsarchiv
D-7480 Sigmaringen
Karlstrasse 3

For the Palatinate:
Staatsarchiv
D-6720 Speyer
Domplatz 6

For Lower Saxony:
Staatsarchiv fuer Niedersaechsen
D-2160 Stade
Am Sande 4C

For southern Germany, Baden-Wuerttemberg:
Hauptstaatsarchiv
D-7000 Stuttgart
Konrad-Adenauerstrasse 4

For Hesse-Nassau:
Hauptstaatsarchiv fuer Hessen-Nassau
D-6200 Wiesbaden
Mainzerstrasse 80

For Brunswick:
Staatsarchiv fuer Braunschweig
D-3340 Wolfenbuettel
Forstweg 2

For Lower Franconia:
Staatsarchiv fuer Unterfranken
D-8700 Wuerzburg
Residenzplatz 2

Appendix   B

ARCHIVES OF THE CATHOLIC CHURCH IN THE FEDERAL
REPUBLIC OF GERMANY

Bischoefliches Dioezesanarchiv Aachen
D-5100 Aachen
Klosterplatz 7

Archiv des Bistums Augsburg
D-8900 Augsburg 11
Hafnerberg 2/II

Archiv des Erzbischoeflichen Ordinariats Bamberg
D-8600 Bamberg
Domplatz 3

Archiv des Bistums Berlin (West)
D-1000 Berlin 19
Wundtstrasse 48-50

Bischoefliches Ordinariatsarchiv
D-8833 Eichstaett
Am Hofgarten

Bistumsarchiv Essen
D-4300 Essen
Zwoelfling 16

Erzbischoefliches Archiv Freiburg
D-7800 Freiburg im Breisgau
Herrenstrasse 35

Bistumsarchiv Fulda im Bischoeflichen
Generalvikariat
D-6400 Fulda
Paulustor 5

Bistumsarchiv Hildesheim
D-3200 Hildesheim
Pfaffenstieg 2

Archiv des Erzbistums Koeln
D-5000 Koeln
Gereonstrasse 2

Bistumsarchiv Limburg
D-6250 Limburg/Lahn
Rossmarkt 4

Dom und Dioezesanarchiv des Bistums Mainz
D-6500 Mainz
Grebenstrasse 8-12

Erzbischoefliches Matrikelamt
D-8000 Muenchen
Pacellistrasse 7I

Katholisches Kirchenbuchamt
D-8000 Muenchen
Bavariaring 24

Erzbischoefliches Ordinariatsarchiv Muenchen
D-8000 Muenchen
Maxburgstrasse 2

Bistumsarchiv Muenster
D-4400 Muenster
Georgskommende 19

Bistumsarchiv
D-4500 Osnabrueck
Hasestrasse 40a

Erzbistumsarchiv
D-4790 Paderborn
Domplatz 3
Postfach 1480

Bischoefliches Ordinariatsarchiv Passau
D-8390 Passau
Residenzplatz 8

Archiv des Bischoeflichen Ordinariats Regensburg
D-8400 Regensburg
Petersweg 11-13

Dioezesanarchiv Rottenburg
D-7407 Rottenburg a. N.
Postfach 9

Bistumsarchiv Speyer
D-6720 Speyer
Kleine Pfaffengasse 16

Bistumsarchiv Trier
D-5500 Trier
Jesuitenstrasse 13b

Bischoefliches Archiv
D-2848 Vechta
Bahnhofstrasse

Dioezensanarchiv Wuerzburg
D-8700 Wuerzburg 1
Domerschulstrasse 2

Appendix   C

ARCHIVES OF THE PROTESTANT AND EVANGELICAL CHURCHES
IN THE FEDERAL REPUBLIC OF GERMANY

Kirchenbuchstelle der Evangelischen Kirche der
Union in Berlin-Brandenburg (Berlin-West)
D-1000 Berlin 12
Jebenstrasse 3

Archiv des Evangelischen Konsistoriums
Berlin-Brandenburg
D-1000 Berlin 21
Bachstrasse 1

Kirchenbuchstelle
D-1000 Berlin 33 (Dahlem)
Archivstrasse 12-14

Evangelische Kirche von Westfalen
D-4800 Bielefeld 1
Altstaedter Kirchplatz 3-5

Braunschweigische Evangelisch-lutherische
Landeskirche in Braunschweig
D-3300 Braunschweig
AlterZeughof 1

Bremische Evangelische Kirche
D-2800 Bremen
Franziuseck 2-4

Evangelisch-lutherische Landeskirche von
Schaumberg-Lippe
D-3062 Bueckeburg
Herderstrasse 27

Evangelische Kirche in Hessen und Nassau
D-6100 Darmstadt
Paulusplatz 1
Postfach 669

Lippische Landeskirche
D-4930 Detmold
Leopoldstrasse 27
Postfach 131

Archiv der Evangelischen Kirche im Rheinland
D-4000 Duesseldorf
Hans-Boecklerstrasse 7
Postfach 10182

Kirchenbuchamt
D-2330 Eckernfoerde
Langebrueckstrasse 13

Evangelisch-lutherische Landeskirche Eutin
D-2420 Eutin
Schlosstrasse 13

Kirchenbuchamt
D-2390 Flensburg
Muehlenstrasse 19

Evangelische Landeskirche im Wuerttemberg
D-7290 Freudenstadt
Lauterbadstrasse 31

Kirchenbuchamt fuer Eiderstedt
D-2556 Garding
Osterstrasse 3

Kirchenbuchamt fuer Niendorf und Pinneberg
D-2000 Hamburg 50
Waidmannstrasse 35

Evangelisch-lutherische Kirche im Hamburgischen
Staat
D-2000 Hamburg
Neue Berg 1

Evangelisch-lutherische Landeskirche Hannovers
D-3000 Hannover
Rote Reihe 6

Evangelische Kirche im Deutschland
D-3000 Hannover-Herrenhausen
Herrenhaeuserstrasse 2A

Kirchenbuchamt Husum-Bredstedt
D-2250 Husum
Schobuellerstrasse 36

Kirchenbuchamt fuer Muensterdorf
D-2210 Itzehoe
Heinrichstrasse 1

Kirchenbuchamt Angeln
D-2340 Kappeln

Evangelische Landeskirche im Baden
D-7500 Karlsruhe
Blumenstrasse 1

Evangelische Kirche von Kurhessen-Waldeck
D-3500 Kassel-Wilhelmshoehe
Heinrich-Wimmerstrasse 4

Kirchenbuchamt Kiel
D-2300 Kiel
Falckstrasse 9

Evangelisch-lutherische Landeskirche
Schleswig-Holstein
D-2300 Kiel
Daenischerstrasse 27-35

Archiv der Evangelischen Kirche im Rheinland
D-5400 Koblenz
Karmeliterstrasse 1-3

Evangelisch-Reformierte Kirche in
Nordwestdeutschland
D-2950 Leer
Saarstrasse 6

Evangelisch-lutherische Landeskirche Hannovers
D-3055 Loccum
Postfach 23

Evangelisch-lutherische Kirche im Luebeck
D-2400 Luebeck
Baeckerstrasse 3-5
Postfach 3034

Evangelische Kirche im Hessen und Nassau
D-6500 Mainz
Steffanstrasse 3

Evangelisch-lutherische Landeskirchenrat
D-8000 Muenchen
Meisterstrasse 13

Kirchenbuchamt
D-2350 Neumuenster 1
Am alten Kirchenhof 8

Kirchenbuchamt fuer Oldenburg/Holstein
D-2431 Neustadt i. Holstein

Evangelisch-lutherische Kirche im Bayern
D-8500 Nuernberg
Veilhofstrasse 28

Evangelisch-lutherische Kirche im Oldenburg
D-2900 Oldenburg
Huntestrasse 14
Postfach 269

Kirchenbuchamt Ploen
D-2308 Preetz
Kirchenstrasse 3

Domarchiv
D-2418 Ratzeburg
Domplatz
Domhof 35

Landeskirchenarchiv
D-6720 Speyer
Domplatz 5

Vereinigte Protestantisch-Evangelisch Christliche
Kirche der Pfalz
D-6720 Speyer
Grosse Himmelsgasse 6

Evangelische Landeskirche im Wuerttemberg
D-7000 Stuttgart 1
Gaensheidestrasse 4
Postfach 92

Evangelisch-lutherische Landeskirche im
Braunschweig
D-3340 Wolfenbuettel
Neuer Weg 88-90

Appendix   D

PORT AUTHORITIES:

Port of Antwerp:

Stadsarchief te Antwerpen
B-2000 Antwerpen, Belgium
Venustraat

   -only the lists for the years, 1854 and 1855 have
survived since World War II.

Port of Hamburg:

Staatsarchiv Hamburg
D-2000 Hamburg 1
ABC-Strasse 19, Eingang A

Museum fuer Hamburgische Geschichte
D-2000 Hamburg 36
Holstenwall 24

   -both of the above will search the lists for a
fee. The Genealogical Department (LDS), 35 North
West Temple, Salt Lake City, UT 84150 have also
filmed the lists and make them available to
researchers via their branch library system
nationwide.

Port of LeHavre:

Archives Nationale de France
F-75141 Paris
60 rue des Francs-Bourgeois

   -the earliest lists, for the years 1749 to 1830,
from LeHavre have been deposited in the Franch
National Library. Latter lists, dating from 1830 to
the present can be consulted at:

Archives de la Seine-Maritime
F-76036 Rouen
Cours Clemenceau

Lists from the Port of Rotterdam were destroyed
during World War II.

Appendix E

MILITARY ARCHIVES IN THE FEDERAL REPUBLIC OF
GERMANY

Deutsches Bundesarchiv
Zentralnachweisstelle
D-5100 Aachen
Kornelimuenster, Abteigarten 6

Geheimes Staatsarchiv Preussischer Kulturbesitz
D-1000 Berlin 33 (Dahlem)
Archivstrasse 12-14

   -maintains a collection of military (garrison)
churchbooks
   and archival sources from East Prussia

Militaerkirchenbuchamt
D-5300 Bonn
Adenauerallee 115

   -Maintains the churchbooks for Catholic military
personnel

Deutsches Bundesarchiv
Militaerarchiv
D-7800 Freiburg im Breisgau
Wiesenthalstrasse 10

   -holdings include military records for Prussia
from the middle of the 19th century to World War II

Kriegsarchiv
D-8000 Muenchen 19
Leonrodstrasse 57

   -military registers from Bavaria

Heeresarchiv
D-7000 Stuttgart
Gutenbergstrasse 109